GOD
iS HERE

Finding God in the Pain
of a Broken World

John W. Nichols

Finding God in the Pain of a Broken World

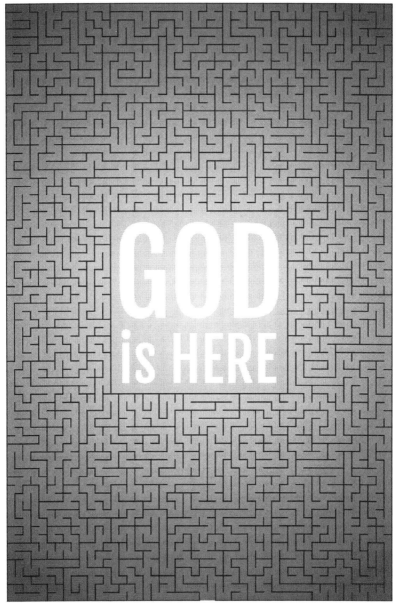

GOD
is HERE

John W. Nichols

Published in Shenandoah, Texas, by God and You and Me CREATIONS.
For information contact : John@GodAndYouAndMe.com

Edited by Joanne Hillman, www.JoanneHillman.com
Cover design and Book Formatting by John W. Nichols
www.GodAndYouAndMe.com/BookHelp
Library of Congress Control Number: 2018911153
Print Edition September 2018 ISBN: 978-1-7328093-0-7
Epub Edition November 2018 ISBN: 978-1-7328093-1-4
Kindle Edition August 2018 ASIN: B07GJY55JF
10 9 8 7 6 5 4 3

Thank you, Trinna, for following the Spirit with me, for pulling me out of my head to laugh and play, for loving our family so well, and for enduring alarms at 3:55 a.m. Thank you most of all, sweet girl, for loving Jesus.

—YOUR JOHN

Contents

For years to come, the debris of a convulsed world will beset our steps. It will require a purpose stronger than any man and worthy of all men to calm and inspirit us. A sane society whose riches are happy children, men and women, beautiful with peace and creative activity, is not going to be ordained for us. We must make it ourselves.

—HELEN KELLER
THE OPEN DOOR[1]

Paradise Lost

What We've Always Wanted

IMAGINE A PERFECT WORLD. Where the evils of crime, hate, and envy are inconceivable—in fact, completely alien. There's no pain, sickness, disease, or disability. No stinging bugs, venomous, or bloodthirsty animals. There aren't even earthquakes, volcanoes, tsunamis, or tornadoes.

In this imagined utopia, motives are genuine. No one has thoughts they can't tell others. We have no misunderstandings and don't need to pretend. Our best foot is always forward because both our feet are perfect. There's constant pleasure. People smile and laugh, freely and unashamedly. Joy overflows each person's heart. Everyone is known and loved. Peace covers the land.

Not only is this ideal society rid of selfishness, it's also rid of poverty. Resources overflow. Every need and want is met. People go to their jobs not merely to scrape by. Occupations are easy, because people are passionate and fulfilled. Their reward is found in the enjoyment of work more than the paycheck.

Whether we recognize it or not, this is what each of our hearts cries for. Why don't we have it?

What We've Had As Long As We Can Remember

When we look at the real world, we see a blurred image of the perfect, tainted with all the opposite characteristics. In the best of times, imperfection lingers and calamity waits at the door. In the darkest times, we cling to the hope that disaster can only last so long.

Even attempting to lead a life of joy and selflessness is draining. Each heart instinctively knows our many anxieties are an injustice. But despite every effort, we suffer.

Faithful friends are rare. Community threatens to shun. We long to be known and accepted, even as we put up walls. Our goodness, we fear, is surely nullified by the hate, impatience, lust, and envy hidden within.

We have impure motives, dirty politics, depression, illness, betrayal, starvation, deformity, natural disasters, perversion, rage, chaos, war, and death—among many other problems. These are the atrocities our hearts cannot understand, the horrors every person desperately wants to escape but has no idea how.

Humanity's made many attempts at solutions, but our problems persist mixed in with the answers. Still lone flowers push out of the asphalt. The starving inexplicably share their bread. Lows turn to highs and back again. We inevitably drink from a diluted, bitter-sweet mixture of heaven and hell on earth.

The Clue In Our Desire

Within our distress is a flickering reality. Every heart desires paradise. Deep down each of us demands things be set right inside and out. We want a place where we are at peace. We yearn for success, prosperity, and abundance of good things. There's an unending search for the fountain of youth where there is promised long life, filled with strength, health, beauty, and vigor. While we can barely conceive undying glee and laughter never squelched, we know we were made for it.

Why does our real world fall short of our dream? What in us longs for utopia? Where does this perpetual longing come from if we've never known its satisfaction?

If we're honest, half the time we don't even know exactly what we want. Despite our disappointment though, we continue to strive without reaching the goal. Only to find when we come close, the mark is moved. There is a clue hidden in all of this though. When our desires aren't met or pain overwhelms us—who do we blame?

The God Problem

In the moment of suffering, we feel we are on our own. Few understand what we are going through. We're helpless and hopeless. No one's there for us, or can help us in meaningful ways. But God could, so why doesn't He?

We wonder, "God, are You with me? And if You're here, do You care I'm hurting? Why did You let me go through this pain? Why aren't You doing something to stop this?"

People blame God for being absent, uncaring, and allowing or even causing disaster, sickness, and death. But it's interesting that we blame Him. Why do these thoughts about God come up? Why do we expect there to be an almighty presence who loves and cares enough to help? The fact that this is our default response proves His existence.

Even zealous believers see tragedy in another's life and think, God has a reason. They have concluded He is using evil for purposes far above our understanding.

Catastrophic events get attributed as God working "for the greater good." Secretly, we avoid such thoughts because the road they lead down is too disturbing. Letting go of certain religious ideas and exploring other answers could unravel our whole approach to life so we avoid them as long as possible.

God's Sense of Humor

Now that I've gotten you thoroughly depressed, I want to lighten things up with a story. Let me set the stage: It was a beautiful day, I was in my early-twenties, walking in the park with two friends—but I had my own metaphorical storm-cloud. I was struggling with a revelation I'd had at church that morning. I felt like God communicated something for me to do, and it involved confessing a sin to someone I had wronged.

I was filled with a mixture of self-abasement, self-pity, and anxiety. My friends knew I was having an internal battle and were giving me some space. We were walking in the same direction, but they were a few feet ahead of me when I tripped, rolled past them, and at the end of my momentum stood up as if I had meant the acrobatic feat. We were all so surprised the only thing we could do was laugh. In fact—it was hard to stop laughing, which made me feel bad for feeling good.

A beam of sunshine broke through my gloom. In the midst of my trial it was possible to find joy. I just needed to open my eyes to see things through a positive light. I'm only human, far from perfect, but do I have to take that fact so seriously? God shook me out of my funk with a reminder to smile. It's all going to be okay.

The Answer

I've asked Him many times, "Where are You, God? Do you even care?" And I've heard people time and time again convey similar doubts. The answer to those questions is, God is close and loves you deeply. He only *seems* distant and aloof. I'm qualified to tell you this, because I've been "far" from God and am now "near." In the midst of overwhelming depression, loneliness, and pain, I experienced God turn my life around. Even as I hated Him for what I had concluded about life, He revealed Himself as good in ways I could not deny.

My focus on the negative in the first part of this introduction was to make a point most of us know all too well—we live in a broken world. Although this was all I could see at one time, my perspective has shifted. I'm more like Tigger than Eeyore now, but it's not because I ignore the pain and suffering around me. It's also not that I have put my trust in the goodness of humanity and our ability.

Helen Keller's quote at the beginning of this introduction said if we want a sane society we must make it ourselves. The truth is we do have responsibility, but each individual needs God to be able to make true positive change in the world. We'll find His Light empowers us to overcome the darkness.

I've encountered God and it was a surprisingly good experience. He's not to blame for our tragedies. In fact, He's the perfect representation of good and is at work in us and around us in amazing ways, beckoning us to join Him.

In this book, I'll share the story of God breaking down my wrong ideas and how He helped me see another perspective. I'll talk about the darkness in us and the world, as well as the Light, and how you can know God's goodness despite the struggles you're facing. My hope is you'll walk away with a peace that defies understanding.

> *Do not be afraid or discouraged, for the Lord will personally go ahead of you. He will be with you; He will neither fail you nor abandon you.*
>
> DEUTERONOMY 31:8 NLT

You've had different experiences than mine, but I believe you're not reading this by accident; and God wants to help you in a similar way as He has me. He wants you to know: at every twist and turn in the maze of life—He's always with you, desperately wanting to help, and never holding back His love.

—JOHN W. NICHOLS

P.S. — The best way to read this book is with the accompanying free workbook and journal. It will help you delve deeper into the questions you're facing in life. For those who want to know more about living for God, being filled with Him, and walking with Him to positively impact the world, I've created a free PDF. Also, in case you prefer to listen to books, I want to give you this book as an audiobook. You can get it all for free (including this ebook) and share it with friends at:

GodAndYouAndMe.com/God-is-Here-Free-Stuff

Darkness cannot drive out darkness: only light can do that. Hate cannot drive out hate: only love can do that.

—MARTIN LUTHER KING JR.[2]

Chapter 1

Inviting God into the Pain

I'M GOING TO ASK you something tough. Trust me though, I'm heading in a positive direction. We're traveling through darkness before reaching the Light. There's darkness in all of our stories.

Remember your worst experience?

Where Was God?

My story begins with a lot of darkness. You've experienced your own, maybe more, but I personally am living proof there's a Light. The pain I struggled with is now stripped of its power. If you're still in darkness as I was, hopefully my story will show you the way out.

The depth of my childhood understanding of God came

from the little bedtime prayer my parents taught me to recite. "Now I lay me down to sleep. I pray the Lord my soul to keep. If I die before I wake, I pray the Lord my soul to take." From a young age, I knew God was somehow involved, but didn't have a deep understanding of Him.

By the time I was four, my parents divorced and my mom started taking me to the Catholic church. I was "confirmed," but my heart wasn't in it. I didn't understand what I was doing, but memorized the words I had to say. Unfortunately, I didn't learn much more about God during this time. I continued calling Jesus "Lord," but it was much later when I actually let Him be Lord of my life.

At around age seven, a friend of the family exposed me to pornography and started molesting me each time I would see him. This went on every other weekend for some time. Fear kept me from telling anyone until I was sixteen. I learned a lifestyle of hiding, lying, and pretending things were okay.

By thirteen, I had trouble relating to others. I didn't have many friends until a group of other loner kids my age took me in and invited me to smoke some pot. Marijuana was my first experience with drugs. I didn't think it was serious, but that didn't stop me hiding it from my parents. I started smoking every day, and it wasn't long before I moved on to other drugs like acid and heroin-based

Ecstasy. This was how I coped with the dark secrets inside me that I didn't want to admit were there.

By sixteen, I started drinking, adding another false comforter. By seventeen, the drugs and alcohol no longer helped cover up the darkness inside. A sea of rage and depression churned beneath the surface. I couldn't see a point i ' living in this harsh world. All I saw was suffering and brokenness. I thought of killing myself, but never seriously tried.

By nineteen, I knew no one could love me if they knew the real me. Despite my hard facade, I wanted understanding, acceptance, and love. I wanted marriage and a family. Later I would realize I sexually objectified women. I had learned to use them and images to satisfy my needs apart from relationship. I never considered the person God made them to be.

I came to believe this world was a big test. At the end of our suffering, God would know if we were good enough for Him. He didn't seem to be present to help, lead, or protect. I hated Him for His apparent absence and indifference. I told Him this in secret too—yelling and journaling accusations against Him.

Where was God when my parents divorced, when I was molested, and when I considered suicide? I couldn't see Him at work in my life or others. Still, I believed He existed—only in a distant, cold place having little to do with us.

The Darkness in Our World

Everywhere we look, we see our society plagued with evil–abuse, theft, murder, human trafficking, war, and so much more. Even apart from people's influence we experience sickness, animal attacks, and natural disasters. If we focus on these things, we might think everything is against us.

Right now, you're facing battles. You may be in a desperate situation such as hopelessness, disability, addiction, debt, divorce, or rebellious children. You've surely had family and friends suffer life-threatening sickness. You've seen loss around you as a result of people's actions and also from random events.

Affliction and trials surround us. Even to take on another's troubles on top of our own is often too much to bear. Trying to help carry someone else's burden takes great faithfulness and selflessness. We may hate to admit this, but it's much easier to shut out the world.

In the midst of these things, God might appear absent. The horrible events around us practically scream out, "If God exists, He's maniacal and cruel!"

The problem—We've become confused and blamed the light for the darkness.

The reason—The trauma of the pain we've faced says we can't trust God. When we turn away from Him our eyes become used to the darkness, and eventually we run from the light.

The solution—We should turn back to God's light, ask Him to lead us out of the darkness, and heal our wounds.

What Happened When I Was Writing

One day, when I was nineteen, I had an experience I couldn't explain. I promise I wasn't high when it happened (it's horrible I have to say that)! However, it was one of the most surreal moments in my life. It was so strange; I wasn't sure what to do.

I was writing in a style called "stream of consciousness," where you compose without thinking. I know many will consider that weird, but it's what I was doing. Now I'm paying for being weird by having to share what happened while I was being weird. Maybe that will encourage you to be normal!

I used to write in this way to be silly and see what off-the-wall things came to me. This was during the time I hated God, but I wasn't thinking of Him in this moment. I was just having fun, minding my own business.

But as I was writing, something changed. In my imagination, I saw a young man from behind and wrote these words as they came to me, "I know you more than you know yourself. And I love you... enough to give my son to die for you." Then the man turned, and I saw he was me.

I thought I was writing from my own perspective looking at someone else. I didn't realize I was looking through God's eyes at myself until He wrote through me, "enough to give my son to die for you." I was absolutely caught off guard by this statement. Remember how I would yell at God and write to Him my angry thoughts? Without warning, God had spoken back. I stopped writing and felt goose-bumps on my arms.

For some months after this happened, I still didn't change a thing. I kept doing drugs. I was still depressed and angry. I didn't want to talk to anyone about God.

I had made conclusions about Him based on experiences and what happened in the world. With my limited ability to make sense of it all, I had determined God was not good. So I hated Him because I didn't understand the true story behind this life.

I share this because, while I had already judged God, He *still* revealed His presence and love. Despite my beliefs, I couldn't ignore that moment. Now, roughly 18 years later, as I've read the Bible and walked in a relationship with God most of that time, I've learned I was so wrong and His character is in line with what happened to me in that strange experience. I can now assure you He loves me, but I'm not more special to Him than anyone else.

Let this be an encouragement for those of you who are praying for God to reveal Himself to someone who seems too far-gone to be rescued. And whoever might not know God personally, I hope my story helps you see how much He wants a real relationship with you. Like He told me, He knows you and loves you... enough to give His son to die for you.

Because of God

Because of God, I am free from drugs, alcohol, and pornography addiction. He's shown me beneath the surface of those things are roots of brokenness in my heart. Although the healing He's bestowed was powerful, it wasn't quick. I'm still learning how to be comforted by Him when I am in pain, feel worthless, anxious, or afraid. But my freedom was impossible without His help.

He's taught me how to recognize what a blessing my parents have been. The ripples of their divorce in 1985 continue today, but He will not stop bringing healing and redemption. In 2006, I was blessed to get married. God is teaching my wife and I how to walk together as two people who have different wounds and different ways of handling pain. He has shown us (both children from broken homes) how marriage is not easy, but with His help it is so good. He opens our eyes to see each other (and ourselves) through His love, hope, faith, grace, mercy, and healing. And He shows us how our differences complement one another. My wife is God's highest blessing to me—after Himself.

He gave us three children, each with a great destiny. Through them, I see the love of His Father-heart, and appreciate my parents who were patient, hopeful, and never raised their voices or hands! He's teaching my wife and I how to trust Him with them.

When my oldest daughter started showing symptoms of Autism, the ideas and conclusions from this book were stress-tested but held. Even though it has been horribly painful—God has shown us His presence, goodness, and words of redemption. We (and our daughter) have faced many trials, but we've also seen miraculous healing. Despite the battles we still face, we continue to believe God for victory.

On top of all this, He has given my family a hope and a future. He's given us a calling, passion, and fulfillment. We are seeing more and more the prayer of Jesus being answered, "Your kingdom come, Your will be done, on earth as it is in heaven" (Matthew 6:10).

God's Will Be Done

Jesus's prayer asks God's will to be done on earth—revealing it is not always done here. In heaven, there is no pain and suffering. They are not God's ways or the inheritance He has prepared for us. And when we let Him in the midst of our darkness, He reveals His kingdom of Light.

Here is a part of the vision of heaven showed in the last book of the Bible:

I saw no temple in the city, for the Lord God Almighty and the Lamb are its temple. And the city has no need of sun or moon, for the glory of God illuminates the city, and the Lamb is its light.

The nations will walk in its light, and the kings of the world will enter the city in all their glory. Its gates will never be closed at the end of day because there is no night there. And all the nations will bring their glory and honor into the city.

Nothing evil will be allowed to enter, nor anyone who practices shameful idolatry and dishonesty—but only those whose names are written in the Lamb's Book of Life.

REVELATION 21:22-27 NLT

The lamb and the light shining for us to see is Jesus. He said, "I am the light of the world. Whoever follows Me will never walk in darkness, but will have the light of life" (John 8:12 NIV).

In Him (Jesus) was life, and the life was the light of men. And the light shines in the darkness, and the darkness did not overcome it.

JOHN 1:4-5 NKJV

Like the light, which scatters the darkness, Jesus is greater than the pain we've faced. The darkness is nothing compared to Him. Despite God's power though, He is humble and rarely forceful. His glorious light is a gentle invitation, bidding us to come out of the darkness, follow Him, and find life.

Let's Pray...

God, please shed Your life-giving light into the dark places in my soul. Reveal to me all that's hiding there— all that belongs to me and all that doesn't. You know the wounded parts of me. Please place Your healing salve on my heart. I may flinch at Your touch, but I know Your balm is what I need. Most of all, let me see You—the real You, the Light of the World, that has never left me. My eyes are used to the dark. Help them adjust to Your Light and follow You, Jesus. So be it!

Next Steps:

1. You're probably reading this book because you're going through some real pain. I'm truly sorry for what you're facing. Although a part of you may not trust Him, take a moment to invite God into the pain and ask Jesus to give you peace.

2. God can handle your honesty about your struggle and your questions. When you think about the negative things you're facing, and have faced in the past, start talking with God about them. Be real with Him. But give Him a chance to speak back to you. Ask Him to show you what He wants to do in those situations. Invite Him to help you and work in your life.

3. As you open up to God, the enemy of your soul watches and knows when you turn toward the Light. He doesn't want you to recognize God. The enemy will work to distract you from Him, and speak false accusations against God. Be wary that you are not believing these lies and accusing the Light for the darkness.

God is in the hearts of all, and they that seek
shall surely find Him when they need Him
most.

—LOUISA MAY ALCOTT[3]

Chapter 2

How to Tell What's True

I CONTINUED MY DOWNWARD spiral for months after God interrupted my writing session. Along the way, a new friend invited me to a Bible-study at a small church in the country. I had been afraid this would happen. From the moment I found out my acquaintance was a church-goer, I was on-guard. I knew eventually he would harass me by talking about God. So of course, I said yes. Wait, what? Nothing in me wanted to agree. But I went. And there God spoke to me again.

In a small drab room surrounded by my enemy (Christians), a quiet string of words went through my mind. Again, I recognized this message was not my own thoughts. Neither was it the subject of the Bible study. I knew the words were only between God and me.

He whispered, "You can think what you want about Me, but it doesn't make it true. If you want to know Me, you need to know what I say about Myself. You need to know My Word."

God gives everything to us by grace, and we receive from Him through faith. "Giving by grace" means the recipient doesn't have to do anything, or be something special to deserve the gift. God's gifts are free and not dependent upon us.

Faith is our response to what God has done and said, even when we can't perceive it as being true with our physical senses. Biblical faith—believing God—isn't only a mental acknowledgement of truth. Faith causes us to act. Sometimes, the action can feel and appear strange because we could have little evidence to support it.

When God said if I want to know Him, I need to know His Word, I had an opportunity to believe and respond in faith. I didn't understand what was happening to me, but a deep hunger came with His whisper.

I started reading the Bible non-stop. I started going to four Bible studies a week, along with Sunday School and church. I couldn't get enough of His Word—a big difference from when I hated God.

Truths and Half-Truths

The quote at the beginning of this chapter from Louisa May Alcott almost get's it right. While it sounds good that God is in the hearts of all, it's an attempt at describing something we can't without God's perspective. Unfortunately, we often try to explain half-truths from our own point of view. We need the whole truth—what the Creator says about Himself and His creation.

Although I will reveal the roots of our troubles and the goodness of God, I'm doing so from a Biblical worldview—meaning rather than using my natural senses and experience to clarify life and God, I use God's Word to interpret it all to the best of my ability.

But knowing the reason for our trials doesn't always ease the pain. Your struggle is valid and your feelings matter. The careful part is how you interpret them. Understanding what's really going on will help you stay in touch with the One who brings comfort.

> **The problem**—We don't know what's true and we judge our experience without all the evidence.
>
> **The reason**—We look at things with our natural senses and try to understand. We can think there's nothing more to life than what's on the surface or we recognize something deeper but don't know how to interpret it.

> The solution—We need God's perspective to teach
> us what's true and how to handle our experience based
> on His truth.

What's Beneath the Surface

From the beach, the ocean appears to stretch towards the horizon without ceasing. I love the panoramic view of water meeting sky with no obstruction. What we can't see, except for occasional hints, is under the deep expanse hides a whole other realm. The ocean is teeming with life you can't know by looking at it from the sand.

Similarly, there's more to our lives than we experience with our five senses. In the same way our eyes can't see deep in the water, our spiritual senses are limited, giving us glimpses we often don't know what to do with.

The problem comes in when we lack God's explanation. Not only as we try to understand spirituality, but when we look at the world, we can't see absolute truth. Everything seems to be in a constant state of flux. Even what feels solid, isn't when you get down to the molecular level. Every conclusion humanity comes to adapts and changes over time.

Quite a bit of our existence is unexplainable. Some say this is spiritual, while others write that off as foolish imaginations and ignorance. But there is a spiritual side of things, and it may be more real than what we perceive with our natural senses.

These muddied views of truth actually come from many sources, which we need a Biblical understanding of. So I'll highlight some of what affects our view of the world and the mysterious elements of our experience.

The Human Soul

Discovering something unexpected about another is one of the joys and dismays in relationships. We've learned to not "judge a book by it's cover" when it comes to people. This is because what makes up a person is more than what you can see on the outside. Our minds house thoughts, emotions, and will—our personality. We aren't just a body and a brain though; there's a spiritual element to us.

When we look in the Bible, we learn God created humanity with at least three different parts. 1 Thessalonians 5:23 shows we have a body, soul, and spirit. Scripture distinguishes spirit and soul, but their differences are often misunderstood.

For the word of God is alive and powerful. It is sharper than the sharpest two-edged sword, cutting between soul and spirit, between joint and marrow. It exposes our

innermost thoughts and desires.
HEBREWS 4:12 NLT

People tend to put up a facade of perfection as much as possible, but every person experiences distress in the realm of the soul. We all have troubling thoughts and emotions, leading to choices with great potential to harm the people we love the most. We exhibit fear, anxiety, depression, and anger. At times, deep down, we feel unfulfilled, ashamed, betrayed, unloved, insignificant, and alone.

The soul is one aspect of life where we only see a part of the picture. Our turmoil can be rooted in past wounds, but these feelings and over-reactions also seemingly come out of nowhere. We explain them away as personality, habits, and sickness or dysfunction in chemical processes. Some might even say, "The Devil made me do it."

The Supernatural

"About three in four Americans profess at least one paranormal belief." This is according to a phone survey of 1,002 adults, conducted by Gallup News Service.[4]

People tell ghost stories, claim relatives have communicated with them after death, and the resuscitated recount tunnels of light and heavenly voyages. Inexplicable help from strangers is received and then the

Good Samaritans can't be found. Not to mention people's belief in ESP, astrology, and witchcraft are just some of the supernatural things people have experienced or believe in.

You're likely to have personal accounts you can't explain too. Maybe a sound in an empty home made your hair stand on end. Have you ever seen someone out of the corner of your eye, or heard a voice calling your name—but no one was there?

When people have experiences like this, we almost always explain them away because they don't make sense. The truth is, we live in a spiritual realm as much as in a natural. We just can't see it most of the time.

Why do cultures everywhere worship gods? Even people who claim there is no God still cry out to Him on their deathbed. Before one of my old friends committed suicide, he wrote a letter saying he hoped the God he questioned existed would forgive him. In grief, our thoughts, and for some reason our requests go to God.

The Spiritual Realm

All these things above point to the fact that we are not only natural beings, but also spiritual. Despite all our science and psychology, something in our very natures assumes there is a God. Without trying, quite automatically, we make judgments about what He is like. But should we use our scales, understanding, senses, and experiences to define God?

Many are trying to explain spiritual truths with the rational mind—even as they're haunted in their inner spiritual dimension—the heart of hearts. There is an emptiness inside and persistent nagging questions about the meaning of life.

Something else hides in the darkness of our pain and suffering. This something—or someone—is the enemy of our souls, an evil force who takes advantage of us when something bad happens. In the darkness he whispers one of two things: "God wasn't with you"—or worse, "God did this to you."

Still another presence, led by God, motivates us in positive ways. This subtle voice in your heart says, "Have hope. It will all be okay. Don't give up! The dawn is coming to chase away the darkness." He whispers almost imperceptibly, "You are valued. You're loved. Your life has purpose."

Good and evil interact with humanity on a regular basis in the midst of our normal lives. But their persuasion is not always obvious. This is simply because we attribute them to ourselves, other people, and chance.

We Have a Part to Play

In life's ocean, we seem tossed to and fro without any control of our own. But the fact is we have a choice. Will we listen to the negative or the positive?

Moment by moment, every person decides which voice they agree with and attune their life to. We make these choices often without recognizing them. Inevitably, our thoughts, feelings, words, and actions follow the one we align with, and our lives are changed for the better or worse.

Whichever force you agree with, the other does not give up pursuing you. The difference is that one pursues to trap, and the other pursues to free. One of the unfortunate lies humanity has believed about God is that He wants to strip us of our freedom and imprison us. But the truth is He has come to remove our shackles.

> *So you have not received a spirit that makes you fearful slaves. Instead, you received God's Spirit when He adopted you as His own children.*
>
> ROMANS 8:15 NLT

> *Now the Lord is the Spirit, and where the Spirit of the Lord is, there is freedom.*
>
> 2 CORINTHIANS 3:17 NIV

We Are Pulled From Both Sides

Even now, after experiencing so much of God's goodness, there are times when I lay my head down at night and a nagging thought haunts me. God, are you going to rescue me? Are you going to come through on my behalf? There's something hiding beneath the surface of this thought. It's a seed of doubt the enemy planted long ago.

This negative thought is a prickly vine rising from the garden of my mind, one that will grow into a spiked, thick tendril if I don't deal with it. It will choke out the good fruit-bearing plants in my life. These doubts about God's presence and goodness will grow if left untended. The distrust starts out small, barely noticeable. And if I let it, this negative perception will grow and cause more damage.

There is also another vine that bears fruit, its seeds scattered by God. Unlike the parasitic plant which destroys, this vine brings sustenance which reproduces life and light. Jesus said, "I am the vine, you are the branches; he who abides in Me and I in him, he bears much fruit, for apart from Me you can do nothing" (John 15:5 NASB).

Another Message

We might overlook these seeds of God's Word— communications of hope, counter to the world's screams against God. Jesus's message is much quieter and less obtrusive. In fact, when it wasn't drowned out by the clamor and busyness of your days, you might have heard the whisper and shaken it off.

The message is this: God loves you.

Sometimes He shows up in dreams or answers simple prayers. Often He brings help through an ambassador in the form of devoted followers. Even seemingly random events can be a blessing from God. He sends these signals all throughout our lives, and we respond in various ways.

Unfortunately we can chalk almost miraculous deliverance up to circumstance. Some will deny His intervention if only so they won't get their hopes up. Some will not recognize His message of love at all because they are so focused on the negative. But some will receive.

For too much of my life I dismissed these communications, a victim unwilling to trust and accept rescue. Like many others who hear of God's love, I chose to ignore it.

Faith

He isn't as obvious as we'd like Him to be. But I believe

that's because He doesn't want to force us to relate with Him. God desires our faith. It's one thing to believe He exists. And another to believe He's good and active in our lives. How forced will it be when He reveals Himself and His glory and majesty causes us to fall down and worship Him? He desires to build a relationship with us now, giving us a genuine choice.

Faith always has room to go to another level. After recognizing the hint of God's presence and interaction with us, faith will lead us to begin to trust Him, see Him for who He really is, respond to Him, become devoted to Him, fall in love with Him, follow Him wherever He leads, and share His message of hope. This is when we become the messenger, sharing God's love with those who do not see it.

I hope you look for these messages and receive them with an open heart. When I came around to recognizing and accepting God's attempts to reach me, my whole life positively changed. I long to see others impacted as I was. The message I once denied, I now humbly deliver to others in need of hope.

But maybe before we get there, we need to hear what God says about His presence and goodness.

Let's Pray...

God, I know I need your perspective. Help me to see life—all my trials, failures, and accomplishments—from Your point of view. Help me to seek and find the truth from You and Your Word. Please forgive me for believing and acting on lies about myself and You. I submit my mind to You, help my ideas line up with what You say. I want to agree with You and not the lie from the darkness. You are worthy of my faith and devotion. Please help me to give them to You every day, no matter what comes my way. In Jesus' name I pray, amen. So be it!

Next Steps:

1. Take a survey of your life, thoughts, emotions, words, and actions and invite God into it all. Ask Him to give you His perspective. The enemy does not want you to talk with Jesus (or anyone else) about what you are going through or have gone through. It will blame God, other people, and yourself in these situations and then inspire feelings of guilt, shame, and that you are utterly alone. A good indicator of which power is at work in your thoughts and emotions is what it would lead to if you believed the idea or feeling. Would it lead you towards God, into the light, and good things, or away from God, into darkness, and bad things?

2. Submit your understanding and feelings to the truth of God. To do this you'll need to schedule regular times of reading God's Word. If you haven't ever read the Bible, a good place to begin is in the Gospel of John in the New Testament. Pick a time of day to spend with God—every day. As you read His word and pray, ask Jesus to reveal the forces at work in the struggles people faced in the Bible. Ask God to help you identify the source of the pain and suffering in your own life history. Did it come from people making bad choices, sickness, or natural disaster?

3. The enemy will try to distract you and/or accuse God, even attempting to use God's Word against Him. The more I read the Bible, the more I understand the context, perspectives of the people, and God's character. The Bible's confusing parts become clear when judged in light of God's goodness, our limited view, and the enemy's corruption. Trust God when what you are reading or experiencing doesn't make sense, and ask Him to show you His truth.

4. As you go through your days, look for God to give you revelations of Himself and truth. He loves to do this, and He is happy to show glimpses of Himself and a greater picture of reality, especially when we seek Him with a genuine heart. When you recognize God's

showing you something, you will be faced with an opportunity to believe or doubt. I encourage you to believe and tell someone who loves Jesus about what God is doing in your life.

"Is he—quite safe?" ...

*"Safe? Who said anything about safe? 'Course he isn't safe. But **he's good**."*

—C.S. LEWIS, THE LION, THE WITCH, AND THE WARDROBE (EMPHASIS ADDED)[5]

Recognizing God's Love and Presence

WHEN LOOKING AT THIS hurting world there are many who say God is either absent or evil. But even for those who've come to the conclusion He's good and active in our lives, at times we feel like He's distant.

You may recognize God's presence in a church service, but how much do you in everyday life? Is God there when you're working, or waiting to see the doctor, or getting your hair cut? What about when you're hurting or when you hurt others—where is God?

I'm here to tell you, whether you recognize it or not, He's always with you. Though you may be running as fast as you can away from Him, He's with you.

He's with you when you are following Him. He's with you when you choose to do something wrong. He's with you when you go to sleep at night and when you wake in the morning.

He is always with you:

> *"God did this so that they would seek Him and perhaps reach out for Him and find Him, though He is **not far** from any one of us. 'For in Him we live and move and have our being.'"*
> ACTS 17:27-28 NIV
> (EMPHASIS ADDED)

> *God is our refuge and strength, an **ever-present** help in trouble. Therefore we will not fear...*
> PSALM 46:1-2 NKJV
> (EMPHASIS ADDED)

> *Where can I go from Your Spirit? Or where can I flee from Your presence? If I ascend to heaven, You are there; if I make my bed in the nether world, behold, You are there.*
> PSALM 139:7-8 NASB

Jesus comforted His disciples before He went to the cross by saying...

> *"I will ask the Father, and He will give you another Advocate, **who will never leave**

you. He is the Holy Spirit, who leads into all truth."

JOHN 14:16-17 NLT
(EMPHASIS ADDED)

But His proximity is not our only concern...

The problem—We don't know how close God is and how much He cares.

The reason—We don't see the true cause of the pain and suffering in the world, and we wonder how a God who is present and good could ever let it happen.

The solution—Ask God to show you His presence, goodness, and love, and thank Him for it.

Okay, okay, He's with me. But maybe I don't want Him to be.

Years ago, when I started reading God's Word, it wasn't long before I realized I was attributing things to God that weren't true. For example, many have the view that God sends bad things our way, for our "ultimate good." Many Bible-educated believers who love God come to this well-meant conclusion.

Without balance the Bible even seems to indicate this in some places. But God has a plan of redemption, taking place over a period of time, and we must look at His Word as a whole. Bear with me, as some of this might be different than what you think or have been taught. I'll give Biblical references as I move forward and do my best to explain how I understand them.

We need to be careful about what we unintentionally blame God for, and what the implications are of the things we attribute to Him. Christians often look at tragedy as if it's from God and somehow a good thing beyond our understanding. When a loved one dies too young, a natural disaster happens, or someone receives a diagnosis of a so-called incurable disease, people try to bring comfort and an explanation with words like:

- God took them home.
- He must have needed them there more than He needed them here.
- God works in mysterious ways.
- He doesn't give us more than we can take.
- He wouldn't have let this happen, unless you could handle it.
- God must be teaching us something.
- God did this to lead us back to Him.
- God disciplines the ones He loves.

Some of these ideas are in the Bible, so there is an element of truth to this. If only because, no matter what happens somehow He works it out for good (Romans 8:28). His goals will be accomplished. He does teach us, lead us, and discipline us. But He does this despite the fallen nature of our world.

Just because He created all we know, is sovereign, and His reign is supreme, doesn't mean He's controlling everything and we're all automatons. Just because He's eternal and knows the beginning from the end and works it all out, doesn't mean He's not with us in the moment, trying to help us and lead us to make the right choices and avoid the wrong ones. Just because He picks up the pieces of our lives and makes art, doesn't mean He smashed them to begin with.

In the next chapter we'll look at some verses that reveal God gave the world to us, but it's under the sway of the enemy and our sinful nature. Before that though, let's see what the Bible says about God, and if He causes our pain and suffering to somehow suit His purposes.

God is Love

God is light and in Him is no darkness at all.
1 JOHN 1:5 NKJV

The Lord is gracious and merciful; Slow to anger and great in lovingkindness.
PSALM 145:8 NASB

The faithful love of the Lord never ends! His mercies never cease. Great is His faithfulness;

His mercies begin afresh each morning.

LAMENTATIONS 3:22-23 NLT

He is patient with you, not wanting anyone to perish, but everyone to come to repentance.

2 PETER 3:9 NIV

The one who does not love does not know God, for God is love.

1 JOHN 4:8 NASB

God—is—love. Consider these famous words about love as if they were talking about God.

Love is patient, love is kind. It does not envy, it does not boast, it is not proud. It does not dishonor others, it is not self-seeking, it is not easily angered, it keeps no record of wrongs. Love does not delight in evil but rejoices with the truth. It always protects, always trusts, always hopes, always perseveres.

1 CORINTHIANS 13:4-7 NIV

If this kind of love is God's pattern for us, how much more does He love in this way? Since 1 John says God is love, let's swap out the word "love" and read the passage from 1 Corinthians again.

"(God) is patient, (God) is kind. (He) does not envy,

(He) does not boast, (He) is not proud. (He) does not dishonor others, (He) is not self-seeking, (He) is not easily angered, (He) keeps no record of wrongs. (God) does not delight in evil but rejoices with the truth. (He) always protects, always trusts, always hopes, always perseveres." Always!

God Gets A Bad Rap

My wife and I have a friend who is hurting so much. She believes God took someone she deeply loved from her when the person got sick and died. She's angry with God and hostile at the mention of Him. I feel so bad for God getting the blame, and our friend is suffering from the lies of the enemy. It's choking the joy out of her life.

I can't blame her though. Before I had a relationship with God, I had a lot of ideas about Him. One was that He sends bad things our way merely for His own cosmic purposes or to test us. This concept is far from the character of God and what is going on in this life. Jesus said, "The thief comes only to steal and kill and destroy; I have come that they may have life, and have it to the full" (John 10:10 NIV).

This full life is Jesus's desire for us, yet people still judge and misinterpret Him. This is as silly as clay questioning a potter (Isaiah 45:9-10), but it happens all the time. If you would like to go deeper into a study of God's attributes, I recommend Andrea Joy Moede's book, Misunderstood:

GodAndYouAndMe.com/Recommends/Misunderstood

He's been misunderstood and falsely accused more than any person who ever lived. But His ultimate goodness gives me confidence to say this—He's better than you could ever hope, dream, or imagine.

The Discipline of God

Becoming a father has helped me get a glimpse of God's love for me. I would give my children anything they wanted if I knew it was good for them. Not only the things I think they should have, or scarcely what they need. I don't even have to like what they want, to enjoy blessing their request. So long as it won't hurt them now or in the future.

And get this, I would *never* make them sick or kill someone to teach them something. This may seem like a ridiculously obvious statement, but for some reason we don't put it past God.

> *"Ask, and it will be given to you; seek, and you will find; knock, and it will be opened to you. For everyone who asks receives, and he who seeks finds, and to him who knocks it*

will be opened.

"Or what man is there among you, if his son asks for bread, will give him a stone? Or if he asks for a fish, will he give him a serpent? If you then, being evil, know how to give good gifts to your children, how much more will your Father who is in heaven give good things to those who ask Him!"

MATTHEW 7:7-11 NKJV

... we had earthly fathers to discipline us, and we respected them; shall we not much rather be subject to the Father of spirits, and live? For they disciplined us for a short time as seemed best to them, but He disciplines us for our good, so that we may share His holiness. All discipline for the moment seems not to be joyful, but sorrowful; yet to those who have been trained by it, afterwards it yields the peaceful fruit of righteousness.

HEBREWS 12:9-11 NASB

I don't know about you, but when I realize I need to change—it's not a nice feeling, and it's rarely easy. But when I discipline my kids it's a good thing, to train them to know how to live. How much better is the heavenly Father's training?

God doesn't discipline with arbitrary punishment and random attacks. All the natural consequences of our actions and everything the enemy throws at us, God will teach us through, turning them around for good and inviting us deeper into relationship with Him and holiness. He trains us purposefully in His ways, bringing peace and righteousness. His primary means of doing that training isn't with trials and suffering, but by His Word.

> *All Scripture is given by inspiration of God, and is profitable for doctrine, for reproof, for correction, for instruction in righteousness, that the man of God may be complete, thoroughly equipped for every good work.*
> 2 TIMOTHY 3:16-17 NKJV

God's True Character

Jesus made this amazing statement that no one is good except for God alone. He basically redefined "good." He didn't use it like we do. We had a good day. Our dog is a good boy when he obeys. The movie was good. She's a good mother. I got a good night's sleep. But Jesus said,

> *"Only God is truly good."*
> MARK 10:18 NLT

What do you think He meant by this proclamation? I've

learned to take Jesus at His word. Let's entertain the idea there is no "bad" in God. To the religious, the mental ascent of this concept is easy, but in many hearts, there are still questions. However, He is truly not like our definition of good. He isn't a mixture, with good ultimately outweighing bad, like we've experienced in life.

We call many things good, despite their imperfections. But Jesus loves perfectly and unconditionally. God's grace is perfect, His generosity towards us immeasurable. Our heavenly Father's mercy, the undeserved pardon we receive, is perfect. His judgment, holiness, righteousness, and purity are good to the point of perfection.

All these characteristics are seen coming together in the life, sacrifice, and resurrection of Jesus. Because God loved the world so much, He humbled Himself and became like us. He did this so He could live the perfect life we were supposed to. Then He gave that perfect life to us graciously, even though we had done nothing to deserve it.

Along with that, God carried out His righteous judgment for our wrong-doings on Jesus, when He went to the cross. Showing God's holiness, but also mercy toward us, because Jesus took the punishment we deserved. Then Jesus conquered death, as God raised Him to new life. And this new life has been offered to us as well.

"For God so loved the world that He gave His only begotten Son, that whoever believes in Him should not perish but have everlasting life. For God did not send His Son into the world to condemn the world, but that the world through Him might be saved."

JOHN 3:16-17 NIV

Who God is With and Who He Loves

"Believers" are those who have placed their faith in Jesus as Lord and Savior. They have received the gift of Him dying for their sins and given their life to Him. Because of this their sins are no longer recognized by God and they have been restored to the relationship their soul has always longed for.

In case you haven't noticed, I'm not only talking to the believers or unbelievers. God is actually with and loves both. Don't get me wrong, I'm not at all saying unbelievers have received the gift of eternal life without submitting to God in faith. I'm not saying when you sin, or aren't following God, there aren't consequences.

But everyone reading this, believer or not, needs to recognize He is with you—always. As long as you have breath, you can't escape His presence, and you can't escape His love. The answer to the question, "Where is God?" is, God is with you. Wherever you are, you can say, "God is here."

In Chapter 1, I had you think back to the worst thing that ever happened to you and asked, "Where was God?" Consider God's character revealed in the verses above. Now, do you see that God was with you on your very worst day, and loving you through it?

Let's Pray...

> God, I want to give You the benefit of the doubt. Even in the turmoil I've encountered, would You show me Your love and presence? Please give me a deeper revelation of Your goodness despite the pain I've faced. Show me the true root of the suffering in this world and my heartache and trials. Forgive me for when I've blamed you for evil. Help me to recognize and thank You for how You're working everything out. Thank You, Jesus, that You give me good things and life to the full. Let it be done!

Next Steps:

1. Invite God to show His true nature to you. As best as you can, lay any ideas you've had about Him down. Over the years I've had many ideas about God and life, which I had to submit to His truth and get His perspective. Ask Jesus for His help and if you've

blamed Him for something He didn't do. Ask Him to show you His goodness and give credit for the good He's done in your life.

2. Ask God if you have attributed any bad things to Him. We don't always recognize when we're doing this. Even so, He loves you and is patient and merciful toward you. Ask His forgiveness for any blame you've placed on Him. In the midst of your trials, He will help you experience His love, joy, peace, patience, kindness, goodness, faithfulness, gentleness, and self-control (Galatians 5:22-23).

3. Look for good things in your life and even good that has come during, or out of, bad things. Start to thank God for the positive. Ask Him to help you continue this habit of recognizing, and thanking Him for the good. When struggles come, remember God's character and thank Him in advance for shifting things to positivity even while you are in pain.

We can easily forgive a child who is afraid of the dark; the real tragedy of life is when men are afraid of the light.

— P L A T O [6]

Chapter 4

Where Suffering Comes From

IF GOD IS SUPREMELY powerful and good, why do we experience the pain we do? Come with me on a journey through God's Word and I'll show you the answer.

> The problem—We don't know who God made us to be, how negative spiritual forces use us, and the depth of God's goodness.
> The reason—We're entrenched in lies we've believed about ourselves, others, and God.
> The solution—Read His Word. Ask God to show you His truth, and begin to exercise faith.

The Very Beginning—The Best Place to Start

When God made mankind, He gave us responsibility in

the world. In other words, before we messed up, when God looked at everything and said it was "good," He allowed people to make choices and even have authority. Many don't want to recognize this, but the Earth has been ours since the beginning.

In Psalm 8:6 (NLT) the writer is speaking to God about humanity and says, "You gave them charge of everything You made, putting all things under their authority... "

Here is the account in Genesis:

> Then God said, "Let Us make man in Our image, according to Our likeness; let them have dominion over the fish of the sea, over the birds of the air, and over the cattle, over all the earth and over every creeping thing that creeps on the earth." So God created man in His own image; in the image of God He created him; male and female He created them. Then God blessed them, and God said to them, "Be fruitful and multiply; fill the earth and subdue it; have dominion over the fish of the sea, over the birds of the air, and over every living thing that moves on the earth."
>
> GENESIS 1:26-28 NKJV

Despite how quickly we learned to shift responsibility (Genesis 3:12-13), authority over the world actually never changed hands. God gave people this dominion without condition. He never said, "I'm giving you authority, until you sin." Or "If you become deceived, I'll take back the control I've given you."

One thing God will not do is go back on His Word. Everything is held together by the power of His Word (Hebrews 1:3), and nothing can break it. Even though God knew we would fail and had a plan for our salvation since the beginning, He instructed the first man, Adam, about humanity's responsibility over the world.

The Bible holds the answer to why the Earth is in such a horrible state. I'm not going to quote all of Genesis (you should read it), but after creating Adam and Eve, and giving them this dominion, He had one rule for them to follow in the Garden of Eden. They sinned when they broke this rule.

Sin is an immoral thing done, or the right thing not done. The ancient Hebrew people who followed God, used the word, sin, in archery. It meant to fail and miss the bull's-eye. Adam and Eve missed the target when they did the thing God told them not to do in the Garden of Eden, eating from the tree of the knowledge of good and evil.

Because of this act of disobedience, an epidemic of sin along with pain and suffering entered this life. Mankind had the perfect utopia we all long for now. But they submitted themselves to evil, and it all went to pieces.

The Enemy

This sin came about when a serpent, later revealed to be a fallen angel named Satan, told Adam and Eve God didn't want them to be like Him (something they already were according to Genesis 1:2), and enticing them to decide what is good and evil apart from God. They fell for the snakes trick and guess what? Humanity continues believing the same lie Adam and Eve fell for.

We are still trying to place ourselves in God's role and determine right from wrong. We continue to give up our God-given authority over the earth. The enemy I mentioned in Chapter 2 controls the world now through people's authority just as he did in the garden. Like Adam and Eve, this happens when we agree with and act on the evil spirit's whispers.

> ... the whole world lies under the sway of the wicked one.
>
> 1 JOHN 5.19 NIV

> And you were dead in your trespasses and sins, in which you formerly walked according to the course of this world, according to the

prince of the power of the air, of the spirit that is now working in the sons of disobedience.

EPHESIANS 2:1-2 NASB

Satan, who is the god* of this world, has blinded the minds of those who don't believe. They are unable to see the glorious light of the Good News. They don't understand this message about the glory of Christ, who is the exact likeness of God.

2 CORINTHIANS 4:4 NLT

*That's a little 'g.' "The god of this world," Satan, has blinded people's minds so they won't believe God and see the truth about Jesus. This serpent has continued to lie about God since the garden.

The Fall of Man and Effects of Sin

God made humanity in His image, sharing some of His qualities with us. In the beginning, He even called us "good" (Genesis 1:31). People reflect God's love, grace, mercy, patience, justice—and goodness. But when Adam and Eve sinned, they died spiritually. From that point on, we've held on to God's standards but lost the ability to live up to them.

If we take a closer look at mankind, we'll find our desire is for good, but we can't escape the evil within us. This is the result of humanity's descent into sinful nature. We've become lost in the darkness which blinded our hearts. Our souls have a vague memory of something called "home." But we can't find it, because sin separates us from our Creator and Father God.

Before recognizing the truth, each person thinks he's on a balancing post. In his mind, he teeters between light and darkness, assuring himself he is good. He struggles not to tip over. But in truth, he already has. He never felt the fall because it happened generations ago in his ancestor, Adam.

> *Therefore, just as through one man sin entered into the world, and death through sin, and so death spread to all men, because all sinned—*
>
> ROMANS 5:12 NASB

The sad but undeniable truth is: Sin permeates the whole world. It's a part of every person's being, so we cannot keep from sinning. Even the most pious people you know struggle with impure thoughts and motives (Jeremiah 17:9-10). No person, apart from God, can escape this.

> *All have sinned and fall short of the glory of God.*
>
> ROMANS 3:23 NKJV

Adam and Eve's personal relationship with God became strained when they chose to sin. They had trusted Satan's deception about God, and in that moment the curse of death entered the world. Romans 6:23 says the punishment for sin is death. This doesn't only mean physical death, but also eternal death—a cutting off from God.

Like a flower cut from the root, Adam and Eve's physical lives began to fade and eventually die from lack of spiritual sustenance. The joy of life and fellowship with God was broken. Sin uprooted their spirits from the source, the Holy Spirit of God.

Ever since, mankind has been born spiritually dead. Every man and woman to this day starts out with the nature of Adam, slaves to sin, under the sway of the enemy, unable to perceive spiritual truth on their own.

Judging Others (But Not Ourselves)

Along with the attacks and temptations from our enemy, we also face the consequences of our own behavior. None of us live up to the standards we believe the rest of the world should, and though we try, we can't blame anyone but the person in the mirror. We rarely recognize this, but it's true. Many times, we see the faults in other people, but we don't in ourselves.

For instance, while in our cars, we judge everyone driving around us. People cut us off, drive too slow, ride our bumper, veer into our lane, and sit too long when the light turns green. Even though we do many of those things too, we believe we drive better than everyone else on the road. We don't drive perfectly though.

Meanwhile, God is absolutely perfect. He would be the only one driving without flaw. Life is much the same way. There's a standard each person strives for and also expects everyone else to meet. But God is the standard-bearer. He created the true rules for living, and He is the only one able to fulfill them.

This is why we all fall short of the perfection our souls long for. The Bible speaks of our hearts as being stone. Until they are reconnected to God, we are unable to have true joy and unconditional love.

Losing Paradise and How to Gain it Back

From childhood, we recognize what life and community should be. It doesn't take long before we learn our ideal is out of reach. But because we don't know the reason, we get angry at the injustice of the world, and blame God.

Sin doesn't only account for the atrocities we see in humanity, but even affects the world around us. This wasn't always the case. In the Garden of Eden, before Adam and Eve sinned, there was no sickness and animals were not threats. I don't believe natural disasters happened before the flood spoken of in Genesis 6.

Our pain and suffering is not God's fault, in fact He has given us a way to get back to the paradise humanity lost. The perfect utopia we imagined in the introduction is a possibility for our eternal future along with the true desire of our hearts. A great Christian named Augustine once said, "You have made us for yourself, O Lord, and our hearts are restless until they rest in you."[7]

The homing beacon in each of us doesn't actually point to paradise—it points to God, and in His presence is paradise. He is the blessing, and with Him comes all the benefits our souls are desperate for.

I saw the Holy City, the new Jerusalem, coming down out of heaven from God, prepared as a bride beautifully dressed for her husband. And I heard a loud voice from the throne saying, "Look! God's dwelling place is now among the people, and He will dwell with them. They will be His people, and God Himself will be with them and be their God. 'He will wipe every tear from their eyes. There will be no more death' or mourning or crying or pain, for the old order of things has passed away."

He who was seated on the throne said, "I am making everything new!" Then He said, "Write this down, for these words are trustworthy and true."

He said to me: "It is done. I am the Alpha and the Omega, the Beginning and the End. To the thirsty I will give water without cost from the spring of the water of life. Those who are victorious will inherit all this, and I will be their God and they will be my children. But the cowardly, the unbelieving, the vile, the murderers, the sexually immoral, those who practice magic arts, the idolaters and all liars—they will be consigned to the fiery lake of burning sulfur. This is the second death."

REVELATION 21:2-8 NIV

The missing element from most dreams of utopia is God. And the terrifying truth is those who don't want His presence will not get it, as He won't force Himself on anyone. But we can't separate life and peace from it's source. Each person must reunite their spirit with the Holy Spirit, and that only comes through God's Son, Jesus Christ.

Let's Pray...

God, thank You for creating every man and woman in Your image. Thank You for giving us dominion over the earth and having a plan to save us even though you knew we would not steward Your gift well. Thank you for not condemning us when we fell away from You. Thank you for loving me and all the world, and sending Jesus despite our faults. I pray You would help me to live in the authority You've given humanity. Help me to take responsibility for myself and my life with Your guidance, protection, provision, and strength. In Jesus' name. Amen!

Next Steps:

1. As best as you are able, continue to soak in the Holy Bible regularly. It is the authoritative Word of God, so we must judge everything from it. Unfortunately, there are a lot of differing applications and interpretations in the world. While navigating these, stay connected to God in prayer and trust Him. He will lead you into all truth.

2. The enemy perverts good things by stealing, killing, and destroying. God gives life—He purifies, generously gives, protects, heals, repairs, creates, and builds. As you read the Gospels, notice Jesus perfectly represents God's character. He said, "I and the Father are one. Whoever has seen Me has seen the Father" (John 14:6-11 paraphrased). Over and over He forgives people and sets them free. Jesus heals the sick, time and time again. In some places it says He healed all who were sick. He even stopped a storm His disciples feared would kill them. Continue to consider the factors at play in Bible stories and what they reveal about God, the enemy, and ourselves.

3. The authority God has granted us in the world is real, but He desires we follow Him as we make choices in word and deed. When we don't we are led by our own desires, ideas, and the sway of our enemy. Take some time to pray and ask God to highlight any areas of your life where you haven't recognized your responsibility or an area you can submit more fully to Him and impact for good. Chapter 6 will help when what you're trying to address is something painful or a personal struggle which is hard to change.

God loves each of us as if there was only one of us.

—AUGUSTINE[8]

Chapter 5

God Wants You as His Child

WHEN I THINK BACK on the words God spoke to me at that Bible-study, I see He wants to be known and loved, even as I do. This thought contradicts many "religious" people's image of God. He, who created everything and is lacking nothing, wants to be known and loved by us? Don't get me wrong, I'm not saying He made the world because He needed us. God had eternal and perfect community in His triune being—the Father, Son, and Holy Spirit.

Still, He wants us. Not only us in general, but you and me specifically. He pushed past my walls and spoke to me one-on-one. He pursues you too, although your interactions with God will be different from mine. No two friends have the same friendship with anyone else. How and what He speaks to us isn't a cookie-cutter experience. Our relationship with God is active, growing, living, and changing as we ourselves mature. And this relationship can bring us into a maturity we never imagined.

Think about my experience. I felt no one could ever love me, if they knew me. But God said, "I know you more than you know yourself, and I love you." Despite His obvious reach towards me, I didn't respond in kind. Did He give up? No, later He put Himself even further in enemy territory and confronted my false ideas. He said, "If you want to know Me, you need to know My Word."

Here I was, only thinking of myself (in the most worldly way). I wanted people around me to understand me, but I especially wanted someone from the opposite sex to know and love me. In the midst of this need, God says, "I know you. I love you."

Ironically, I hated God for what I thought I knew about Him. But He never stopped loving me. Most of us will not find it easy to get over being falsely judged and accused. But when I misjudged God, He showed me mercy and didn't write me off. He invited me to know Him instead!

God is so misunderstood. I had no concept of His unconditional love and goodness. I've come a long way in this wonderful relationship, but I've probably still only scratched the surface. I truly believe it's impossible for us to imagine the depth and perfection of His unconditional love.

Coming into the Light

God cares about your struggles and wants to walk with you through them. He wants to be known by you—and to be loved. He doesn't give up on you as long as there's a chance for your relationship to grow. As long as you have breath, His love always hopes and always perseveres.

When I took God up on His invitation to know Him and started studying the Bible, I began feeling an urgency which grew until I couldn't ignore it. My relationship with God was becoming real and healthy. He had planted a spiritual seed inside me and the vine of life and light was breaking out of its shell.

It wasn't long before I gave in and surrendered myself to the Lord. I longed for my whole being to be consumed by Him, for the darkness to be washed away, to be saturated and filled to overflowing with light, to discard my old dead way of being, and be born again with new life.

For you were once darkness, but now you are light in the Lord. Live as children of light (for the fruit of the light consists in all goodness, righteousness and truth) and find out what pleases the Lord. Have nothing to do with the fruitless deeds of darkness, but rather expose them. It is shameful even to mention what the disobedient do in secret. But everything exposed by the light becomes visible—and everything that is illuminated becomes a light. This is why it is said: "Wake up, sleeper, rise from the dead, and Christ will shine on you."

EPHESIANS 5:8-14 NIV

The problem—We're not convinced God really wants us.

The reason—Deep down there is a feeling of unworthiness in us, that tells us we're not lovable.

The solution—Ask Jesus to make the perfect love of the Father real and personal to you.

The Gift of Jesus—The Light of the World

We often make the mistake of feeling like God can't relate with our suffering. But Jesus went far out of His way to show His love and understanding. He truly cares about everything you've faced.

He was despised and forsaken of men,
A man of sorrows
and acquainted with grief;
And like one from whom
men hide their face
He was despised,
and we did not esteem Him.
Surely our griefs He Himself bore,
And our sorrows He carried;
Yet we ourselves
esteemed Him stricken,
Smitten of God, and afflicted.
But He was pierced through
for our transgressions,
He was crushed for our iniquities;
The chastening for our well-being
fell upon Him,
And by His scourging we are healed.
All of us like sheep have gone astray,
Each of us has turned to his own way;
But the Lord has caused
the iniquity of us all
To fall on Him.
ISAIAH 53:3-6 NASB

For we do not have a High Priest who cannot

sympathize with our weaknesses, but was in all points tempted as we are, yet without sin. Let us therefore come boldly to the throne of grace, that we may obtain mercy and find grace to help in time of need.

HEBREWS 4:15-16 NKJV

Despite how all of us are infected with a sinful nature, as we discussed in the last chapter, Jesus looked past our imperfections and came to us. Even so, many feel they can't be right with God. If only the truly righteous can enter His presence, what hope do we have?

God knows all things. From eternity He saw we would fail in our responsibility to rule over His creation while walking with Him. He knew in advance humanity would sin, and instead of ditching us, He planned our rescue. God's creation Adam ushered darkness into our existence, but He broke the curse by sending His son Jesus, the Light of God.

For since death came through a man, the resurrection of the dead comes also through a man. For as in Adam all die, so in Christ all will be made alive.

1 CORINTHIANS 15:22-23 NIV

God's word could not be broken, and He set mankind

(with free-will) in charge of this world. So to accomplish our redemption, almighty God humbled Himself to become like us. The Bible says Jesus was the fullness of God in human form. He was not merely a man, but God in the flesh.

Because of this, Jesus was the only human who could repair our mess. He was the only one able to tip the scales of righteousness. No one else has been able to live a perfect life without sin. The amazing truth is, before God even created the world, Jesus took our death sentence so we could be right with the Father (Revelation 13:8).

Everything was created through Him and for Him. He existed before anything else, and He holds all creation together. Christ is also the head of the church, which is His body. He is the beginning, supreme over all who rise from the dead. So He is first in everything.

For God in all His fullness was pleased to live in Christ, and through Him God reconciled everything to Himself. He made peace with everything in heaven and on earth by means of Christ's blood on the cross.

This includes you who were once far away from God. You were His enemies, separated from Him by your evil thoughts and actions.

Yet now He has reconciled you to Himself through the death of Christ in His physical body.

As a result, He has brought you into His own presence, and you are holy and blameless as you stand before Him without a single fault. But you must continue to believe this truth and stand firmly in it. Don't drift away from the assurance you received when you heard the Good News.

COLOSSIANS 1:16B-23A NLT

But Satan continues to whisper, "the Light (Jesus, God, Christianity, redemption) is a lie." Ironically, he is the one who distorts all truth. The enemy blames God for every trial, even as he twists the knife in our heartache. Satan tells us God doesn't want us to enjoy life and perverts His beautiful gifts—friendship, marriage, parenthood, intelligence, creativity, etc.

The enemy has been telling the same lies about God and about humanity ever since the Garden of Eden. Chief among them is, "You can't trust God and you need to live apart from Him." But God continually gives mankind the opportunity to believe Him and become His children again. You get to decide who to listen to. Will you accept what Jesus did for you?

The Abusive Father

As long as we reject God's fatherhood, we may think we are free, but there is another spirit who seizes God's rightful position in our hearts. Jesus warned the unbelieving Jews of this when He said they imitated their true father:

> *They replied, "We aren't illegitimate children! God Himself is our true Father."*
> *Jesus told them, "If God were your Father, you would love Me, because I have come to you from God. I am not here on my own, but He sent me. Why can't you understand what I am saying? It's because you can't even hear me! For you are the children of your father the devil, and you love to do the evil things he does. He was a murderer from the beginning. He has always hated the truth, because there is no truth in him. When he lies, it is consistent with his character; for he is a liar and the father of lies."*
>
> JOHN 8:41-44 NLT

Jesus never ceases to amaze me. In the quote above, He's talking to the religious leaders of the Jewish culture. He straight up told them, their daddy was the devil! Not only does this give us insight into the devil (he is "the father of lies"), but it also reveals something amazing and frightful. Jesus was not just name-calling. These people had no idea they belonged to their father the devil.

I referenced Ephesians 2:1-2, in the last chapter, when talking about how the world is under the sway of the enemy. It says Satan's "spirit is now working in the sons of disobedience." The word "sons" isn't written as merely poetic language. Everyone since Adam was born into this spirit's sonship. It comes along with the plague called our sinful nature.

If Jesus were to call you a "son of disobedience" or a child of the devil, you'd either feel hopeless or hostile. But what if He said it with love, mercy, grace, and an offer of freedom? The Great Physician lets us know our condition and the way to be healed.

Our condition will kill us eternally, but God made a way to pay for sins through the bloodshed and death of something innocent (Leviticus 17:11, Hebrews 9:11-18). Jesus's sacrifice on the cross was the ultimate payment for the sins of the world.

Father God loosed Satan's bonds on us by paying for our freedom with the life of His willing Son—Jesus.

Finally Adopted!

God decided in advance to adopt us into His

own family by bringing us to Himself through Jesus Christ. This is what He wanted to do, and it gave Him great pleasure. So we praise God for the glorious grace He has poured out on us who belong to His dear Son. He is so rich in kindness and grace that He purchased our freedom with the blood of His Son and forgave our sins.

EPHESIANS 1:5-7 NLT

For there is one God and one mediator between God and mankind, the man Christ Jesus, who gave Himself as a ransom for all people...

1 TIMOTHY 2:5-6 NIV

For all who are being led by the Spirit of God, these are sons of God. For you have not received a spirit of slavery leading to fear again, but you have received a spirit of adoption as sons by which we cry out, "Abba! Father!" The Spirit Himself testifies with our spirit that we are children of God, and if children, heirs also, heirs of God and fellow heirs with Christ, if indeed we suffer with Him so that we may also be glorified with Him.

ROMANS 8:14-17 NASB

God knew no human would be able to live up to His

standards, so He met them for us. Jesus lived a sinless life, and was punished in our place, so our spirits could join with God. Those who put their faith in Jesus, He spiritually positions in His death, and raises us with Jesus into His life. From that point God considers us His children.

God loves us. He extends the chance to experience the life we long for and the one He meant we live. He offers us the adoption papers, but we must take them, and put our lives in His hands. The Bible is clear: to get to be with God in heaven, you must receive Jesus's work on the cross. God did His part. We can either deny or accept this gift.

If you haven't surrendered to God, I earnestly pray you will. Even though He doesn't stop pursuing us in this life, the Bible indicates we can only make the choice while we live in this world (Hebrews 9:27, Matthew 7:21-23, Luke 16:19-31). We never know when our time here will be up, and then we will either be eternally with God who is good, or eternally separated from Him by our own choosing.

If you want to receive what Jesus did for you, turn your life over to Him. Agree with Him that you have not lived in His ways, and turn away from sin to follow Jesus the rest of your life. Believe God raised Him from the dead, and He will raise you too.

Jesus's salvation is a free gift to those who have faith. Giving yourself to Him and receiving God's adoption as

His own child will save your soul as well as your life in this world. You will never be the same!

In case you would like to read more about salvation, what happens when you are born again, and what to expect after being saved, I've written a PDF appendix on giving your life to Jesus, being filled with the Holy Spirit, and walking with the Spirit. This is included with the free workbook and audiobook here:

GodAndYouAndMe.com/God-is-Here-Free-Stuff

If you gave your life to God before reading this book, He's always inviting you to dive deeper. Because of God's unending depth, we can have an ever-deepening relationship with Him. I submitted myself to God a long time ago, but I continue giving more of my life to Him, and experiencing the greater abundance He created me to enjoy. Your devotion and love for God will grow as you continue to receive His endless love for you.

Let's pray...

Jesus, thank You for showing me You care about our suffering and this human existence by coming to live as a man. You experienced temptation and the pain we go through first-hand. Thank you doing that without fault, and then laying down Your life for me, even though I was a child of disobedience. God, thank you for choosing me in love as a Father, and not grudgingly. I'm so thankful you loved and accepted me with all my faults, and you aren't leaving me broken. Despite my unloveliness, you have lifted me up and transformed me into a different person. Thank You for giving me Your Holy Spirit, who reminds me I am Your child. Please help me live every day with these truths in mind. Please show me Your healing power in every part of my life. So be it!

Next Steps:

1. As best as you can, start recognizing God is the perfect Father—He really is good. Even if you had a negligent, domineering, or abusive father, you have a heavenly Father who loves you unconditionally. During your regular scheduled times of reading the Bible (discussed in the Next Steps of Chapter 2) make sure to not just read the Bible, but take time to spend with God. Approach God as a beloved child coming to your attentive Father. Talk one-on-one with your Daddy, unloading all you're going through, all your needs, and even the desires of your heart. He cares about everything you're struggling with and all the things you think throughout your day.

2. As you're spending time with Him, quiet your soul and listen for His response. One of the first times I recognized God speaking to me during a quiet time, He said, "I love you," the most precious words anyone can hear. It wasn't audible, but in my spirit I recognized

the words. Sometimes He speaks simple encouragement like this. Sometimes He gives direction and wisdom. Sometimes He corrects. But He never condemns.

3. When God speaks, you have an opportunity to believe or doubt. Everyone wonders if they really heard God, if it was their own voice, or even the enemy's. Some criteria to know if God's speaking to you is: Does what you "heard" line up with His character and the Bible? Is it something you would think, or do the words contain a wisdom beyond you? Will it produce good things if you accept and act on it? The more you take time to do this, you will get a better grasp on how God speaks to you, and how to follow His leading. He is the perfect Daddy and has the best plans for you, His child.

There is no more devastating blow against evil than when a human being chooses God in the face of suffering, disappointment, unbelief, chronic pain, frustration, abandonment...
Before the circumstances change, to get up and proclaim that God is good is a devastating blow to evil.

—JOHN ELDREDGE[9]

Chapter 6

Finding True Comfort

Your soul is wounded, pierced by a flaming arrow from our enemy. Whether this injury is fresh or old, doesn't change the haunting anguish. The echo of the strike threatens to never stop reverberating in your memory.

Sometimes it's from the betrayal of the one you trusted. Sometimes it's the tragedy of a loved one dying young. Sometimes it's the simple disappointment of a hope deferred or a trial that never ends.

He heals the brokenhearted and bandages their wounds.
PSALM 147:3 NLT

The promise of God is to heal our hearts. But from the

moment these attacks hit us as children, we begin seeking a semblance of peace, joy, fulfillment, and comfort. Often we haven't learned how to get these things from the only One who can truly give them. Not only do we fill these holes with bad things like illicit drugs or binge drinking, but also through perversions of good things like relationships, food, shopping, entertainment, hobbies, work, and achievements. In the midst of suffering we're more tempted than ever to take our eyes off Jesus.

Practices become ingrained, and we try to convince ourselves there's not a problem. Until we realize they're only band-aids for the gaping wounds we have. Somehow the enemy keeps us chasing answers apart from God.

The reason drugs and alcohol are popular is we want a break from the pain of life. Many people say their use is just social and recreational, simply the fun of being inebriated. But the bottom line is many more use them for comfort.

Even after giving my life to Jesus, I kept trying to escape reality. Soon the Bible taught me illegal drugs weren't something I should be doing! The Holy Spirit's conviction overcame me, and I wanted Him alone to be my comfort.

This destructive habit was hard to shake, and it was merely the external problem. The real issue was I had no idea how to let God meet my needs. It was easier to cover my shame and avoid the pain than to seek God for a deep work of healing.

Quitting drugs wasn't easy for me. I seemed to have no power to overcome the addiction. When my old friends offered them to me, it was as if I didn't have a choice. I finally asked them to not get high around me, which didn't work. Even when some friends tried, I had forgotten how to have fun while sober.

God has instantly set people free from drugs, even healing withdrawals and cravings miraculously, but that wasn't my experience—maybe because I only believed and acted in my own strength. I hadn't yet had a powerful encounter with the One who Jesus called "another Helper."

"And I will ask the Father, and He will give you another Helper (Comforter, Advocate, Intercessor — Counselor, Strengthener, Standby), to be with you forever—"
JOHN 14:16 AMP[10]

The problem—We try to handle things apart from God, but we're powerless when confronted with sin, cravings, broken-heartedness, persistent sickness, and soul-level affliction.

The reason—We live and are led by intellect, feelings, and our bodies instead of the Holy Spirit of God. We don't believe we're capable of change, and we go to God for our comfort last.

The solution—Believe the truth in Scripture about our inheritance, freedom, and potential with the help of the Holy Spirit. Ask God to teach you to be led by the Spirit, reveal the work of the Spirit, and fill you with His Spirit. Repent and renounce sin, break free from its clutches, and stop practicing it.

The Spirit of God in You

Imagine a superhero who never discovers his powers or is convinced not to use the gifts he has. This protagonist goes through life seeing the darkness around him, believing the lie that he's incapable of making a difference. How sad and frustrating to be on the outside looking in on this situation. We know of his potential but watch him shrink back, hide, and act like any normal person. Instead he should fight the evil in his own life and in the lives around him.

Most Christians live like this not-so-super hero, very similar to the rest of the world. Meanwhile there's something extraordinary within. I say "something," but I should say Someone—the Holy Spirit of God.

If the Spirit of Him who raised Jesus from the dead is living in you, He who raised Christ from the dead will also give life to

*your mortal bodies because of His Spirit who
lives in you.*

ROMANS 8:11 NIV

I finally experienced transformation when I believed AND acted in the truth of this resurrection power living in me. The things we struggle with are nothing compared to the power of Him who brought Jesus out of the grave.

After the culmination of my struggles, there are still those long, hard days where old habits whisper I need something to take the edge off—just a little distance and distraction from the pain to get me through the night. That's when I dig deeper and invite the Comforter into the midst of my troubles, saying "What's the root of this, Holy Spirit? Why is this harder than it should be? Where do I need You to shine your light?"

If Jesus were next to me, I could lay my head on His chest like the disciple who He loved. But the Son of God did say, it's better that He goes so the Helper can come (John 14:6). We know from His other words that Holy Spirit dwells within us and never leaves. As difficult as it is to believe, it is actually better for Him to be in us, than for Jesus to be by our side.

When my Counselor reveals where I need healing, even as I can't describe my anguish, I invite Him to bring His peace, comfort, and redemption.

And the Holy Spirit helps us in our weakness.
For example, we don't know what God wants
us to pray for. But the Holy Spirit prays for
us with groanings that cannot be expressed
in words. And the Father who knows all
hearts knows what the Spirit is saying, for
the Spirit pleads for us believers in harmony
with God's own will.

ROMANS 8:26-27 NLT

In a similar way, I've learned to trust Him for guidance, help, and strength—even the ability to minister to others. He's given me wisdom and words people needed which I couldn't have known, I've seen miraculous healing in my family, and He's helped me to walk in a calling I never thought I was capable of.

"Eye has not seen, nor ear heard,
Nor have entered into the heart of man
The things which God has prepared
for those who love Him."
But God has revealed them to us through His
Spirit. For the Spirit searches all things, yes,
the deep things of God. For what man knows
the things of a man except the spirit of the
man which is in him? Even so no one knows
the things of God except the Spirit of God.

Now we have received, not the spirit of the world, but the Spirit who is from God, that we might know the things that have been freely given to us by God.

These things we also speak, not in words which man's wisdom teaches but which the Holy Spirit teaches, comparing spiritual things with spiritual.

1 CORINTHIANS 2:9-13 NKJV

Since God's Spirit dwells with ours when we are born again, we are now able to fulfill what Jesus said in John 4:24—"worship in the Spirit and in truth." Worshiping God in Spirit is both the easiest thing to do and the most difficult.

The hardest part is we're utterly used to living according to our own strength—our own efforts, our own understanding, our own feelings, and our own desires. And we may want a rational explanation, as well as an emotional or physical sensation, to confirm spiritual experiences. Unfortunately this concept and bad teaching is what held me back from walking in the power of the Spirit for many years. Though there are times when God gives divine revelation alongside understanding and sensations, we shouldn't require this to worship in Spirit.

On the flip side, this is why worshiping in Spirit is

easy: no matter how we feel, we are strong in Spirit. It's above reason and counterintuitive, but all we need is faith, freedom, and rest in God. We simply must believe His Word, receive His promises, and walk with Him in peace.

The Things We Need to Turn From

I was haunted by the Holy Ghost the last time I did acid. I had started following Jesus (shocking, I know, considering my behavior), and as the chemicals went through me, my every thought turned to God. I couldn't escape Him. I kept thinking something like, "Depart from me, for I am a man of unclean lips" (Isaiah 6:5). Only He and my unclean lips wouldn't leave me alone.

Thankfully, that experience with acid was horrible. I became aware of an odd mixture of pride and shame within—as well as selfishness and sarcasm. For the first time, I didn't like being out of control. So I trashed what I'd saved for later, asked God to forgive me, and told Him I wouldn't do it again.

In that moment I had unknowingly repented and renounced my sin. You too can kick your habit. Whatever you're going to for comfort, put it in its rightful place and proclaim you're not going back to it for relief.

Those things grip us because they're agreements we've

made with lies from our enemy. When we're struggling, our captor baits his cage with whatever tells us we can find peace. Repenting and renouncing sin is accepting Jesus's truth, breaking out of our shackles, and then chasing off the enemy with a loud roar.

The Meaning of Repentance and Renunciation

Repentance is turning away from the wrong path and taking the right one. Think of it as obeying your GPS navigation's instructions, "Recalculating... Make a U-Turn." It means completely changing course.

It's more than saying, "Sorry, GPS. You're right, I went the wrong way. I'll stop here." That voice will keep bugging you until you shut it off or get back on the right track. I didn't just quit drugs. I needed to also go to God for healing, comfort, peace, and joy.

Renouncing is making a declaration of independence and taking ownership of whom you will be submitted to. It's not enough to desperately say, "Please, self, stop doing wrong things." That attitude of powerlessness does not inspire mercy in the enemy, your flesh, or your soul still needing redemption. It leaves your focus on your weakness and what you're attempting to avoid, rather than the power of God.

Instead, let's boldly declare, "I am not a slave anymore to _____!" Then believe and act like it's finished.

Practicing repentance and renunciation is a key to experiencing freedom and victory on this side of heaven. Because of the Holy Spirit, who is at work in you, you're stronger than you think or feel.

God's Word About Your Transformation is True

Many Bible verses which include a derivative of the word "renounce" have to do with renouncing God—a big no-no. But in 2 Corinthians, Paul applies it to the sin we're leaving behind and the ministry we're heading toward.

> Now the Lord is the Spirit, and where the Spirit of the Lord is, there is liberty. But we all, with unveiled face, beholding as in a mirror the glory of the Lord, are being transformed into the same image from glory to glory, just as from the Lord, the Spirit. Therefore, since we have this ministry, as we received mercy, we do not lose heart, but we have **renounced** the things hidden because of shame, not walking in craftiness or adulterating the word of God, but by the

manifestation of truth commending ourselves
to every man's conscience in the sight of God.
2 CORINTHIANS 3:17–4:2 NASB
(EMPHASIS ADDED)

Scriptures which use the word repent are more common. Here's one great example:

"Repent, then, and turn to God, so that your sins may be wiped out, that times of refreshing may come from the Lord..."
ACTS 3:19 NIV

These show it's possible to escape the trap of a harmful lifestyle.

You won't spend the rest of your lives chasing your own desires, but you will be anxious to do the will of God. You have had enough in the past of the evil things that godless people enjoy—their immorality and lust, their feasting and drunkenness and wild parties, and their terrible worship of idols.
Of course, your former friends are surprised when you no longer plunge into the flood of wild and destructive things they do. So they slander you. But remember that they will have to face God, who stands ready to judge

everyone, both the living and the dead.

1 PETER 4:2-5 NLT

... just as you presented your members as slaves of uncleanness, and of lawlessness leading to more lawlessness, so now present your members as slaves of righteousness for holiness.

ROMANS 6:19 NKJV

Maybe you're convinced you can't shake your addiction. The truth is that God is stronger than whatever has a grip on you, and He's made it possible for you to overcome. Turn towards Him, and literally speak out a declaration in faith, "_____ has no power over me! I renounce it in Jesus's name!"

Your belief that these verses are true is vitally important. I dare you to take off the grave clothes you wore on the path that leads to death and put on the righteous robes Jesus's cross bought for you. Turn to the living way He redeemed you for when you put your faith in His resurrection. Stop agreeing with the lies shouted at you by your old prison guard. Start declaring the truth first spoken by the One who set you free.

Let's Pray...

> God, I declare Your Word is true. Help me to also act like it's true in faith. I confess I medicated pain in my own strength instead of choosing Your healing. Please forgive me for looking elsewhere to meet my needs. I now set my eyes on You. (Say this out loud and boldly) I turn away from _____ and pull up its roots, in Jesus name! I command every spirit I've listened to who is not the Holy Spirit, to go, in Jesus name! I pray, God, that You would pour out a fresh anointing of Your Holy Spirit on me and fill me to overflowing. Help me to live in the freedom Jesus bought me and to worship You in Spirit and in Truth. Amen!

Next Steps:

1. If you feel like the Holy Spirit and His gifts are mysterious, or if you're leery about this kind of stuff, I can relate. For years, I felt the same. If this is where you are at, or you're just interested in reading more about the Holy Spirit, I recommend you download my free PDF from:

   GodAndYouAndMe.com/God-is-Here-Free-Stuff

2. As you come across verses in the Bible about what Jesus has done for you as a believer, take a moment to pray and ask the Holy Spirit to help you live in the truth of His Word. (There is more about this in the next chapter.)

3. Although you are truly free, part of yourself is still in the process of positive change. The enemy will try to convince you of your bondage. When you realize this, continue to renounce Satan's lies and turn toward God for healing and redemption. Keep coming back to God, asking Him to speak and inviting Him deeper.

4. If a quick change isn't evident and you continue to feel weak, don't be discouraged. The Word of God is like a seed, which often takes time to grow and bear fruit. Continue to cultivate and practice His truth in your life, expecting victory. Often, this is a process and not a one-time event. Let even that make you glad, because you must humbly rely on the Holy Spirit, your Best Friend and Comforter. His strength is absolutely revealed in your weakness.

God has been good and He will continue to manifest His goodness. Let us approach these days expecting to see the goodness of the Lord manifest. Let us be strong and of good courage, for the Lord will fight for us if we stand in faith.

— FRANCIS FRANGIPANE[11]

Chapter 7

How God Changes Everything

I STARTED THIS BOOK focusing on a few common questions about life and God. At every twist and turn in the maze of life—why is there so much turmoil? Where is God? Does He care? The boiled-down answers are: we are responsible for this world but there is a negative spiritual force at work, still, God is here and active with us, and His personal love and goodness are immeasurable.

When you love God in return and submit yourself to His ways, He is able to complete His good plan for your life, despite your mistakes and the fallen nature of this world. He's always been present and active in your life (even before you recognized Him), attempting to redeem every part so you would come to know and rely on Him.

God's brought so much healing to me. I feel like the

wounds I received and inflicted on myself are from a different life or even another person's story. I wasn't immediately healed though; it took time. And I've continued to face various trials, some brought on by my own mistakes, and some from the enemy and broken world we live in. But as I've learned to constantly walk with God through hardships, I've experienced breakthrough. Sometimes in the quick and miraculous ways where you can't deny it was God, but more often in the day-to-day interactions with Him and His people, that bring change over time.

How Should We Interact with God?

Even when people haven't acknowledged God, He has acted in the world and brought about good things. He wants us to recognize Him, and give Him the honor He deserves, but He doesn't need us intrinsically. In fact, He's been at work since before time as we know it—amazingly working on our behalf before He had even created us.

He (Jesus) was foreknown before the foundation of the world, but has appeared in these last times for the sake of you who through Him are believers in God, who raised Him from the dead and gave Him glory, so

that your faith and hope are in God.
1 PETER 1:20-21 NASB

"I am the Alpha and the Omega, the Beginning and the End, the First and the Last."
REVELATION 22:13 NKJV

"Then the King will say to those on His right, 'Come, you who are blessed by My Father; take your inheritance, the kingdom prepared for you since the creation of the world.'"
MATTHEW 25:34 NIV

God has been active since the beginning and thankfully many see Him working in their lives, but it's important to consider what our relationship to Him should be like. Can we interact with God? What happens when we talk to Him? Can we experience Him in a meaningful way?

Even though I prayed before I was a Christian, I didn't think much about how I spoke to God or if He might speak to me. I said prayers I had memorized from childhood, prayers from my culture, involuntary cries for help, and plenty of accusations.

When I gave my life to the Lord, I struggled with feeling very formal and religious while praying. I didn't know how to talk to Him. I wanted to treat God as my Father and see myself as His son. But I found my tendencies were to address Him like a peasant before an emperor.

I fear the Lord in the Biblical sense, in other words, His perfect holiness demands respect. I recognize He is great, mighty, awesome, completely pure, and a righteous Judge and King. But He is not a tyrant who rules subjects from a distance. Jesus shows us that God is a King who eats with His people and gives His life on the front-line of battle.

God is not the kind of Father who works twelve hours, and then goes to a bar to avoid His family. He doesn't fly off the handle with His children and become abusive. He is a Father who communicates, provides, teaches, plays with, protects, and holds His children.

So I do regard God in high esteem, but I have to remember my standing has changed because of Christ. Where I used to be an enemy, I am now God's child and He invites me into the throne room, even to sit beside Him just as Jesus does (Ephesians 2:6-7).

> Let us therefore come boldly to the throne of grace, that we may obtain mercy and find grace to help in time of need.
> HEBREWS 4:16 NKJV

Talking with God, in a relational way, wasn't intuitive. But eventually, I learned to converse with Him the way I would a friend. I guess it makes sense when you think about talking with someone who you have baggage with. If you keep at it, there will come healing, and then eventually an ease and friendship. I kept going to God, like working on a strained relationship. Obviously, this relationship was not damaged by Him, but my own misguided perception of Him.

Practically, it looked like disciplining myself to have early morning times tucked away to pray and read my Bible. I talked with Him first in regular set-aside times of devotion like this, but now I'm also in constant communication as I go through my day. I still pray in the quiet-place, but I continue submitting my thoughts to Him as well, while doing my best to listen and follow Him everywhere I go.

The sooner you can talk to Him in a non-religious way, the sooner you will recognize the personhood of God. He is a person who loves you, His child, as a perfect Father *who feels*. If we look, we'll find God exhibits emotions in the Bible. He gets jealous over His people. He laughs. He cries. God is not mechanical. He is not tame. He is the living God, who desires a deep and intimate connection with you.

God and You and Me

His relationship with you is very personal, but believe it or not, it's also meant to change the world. Since you've received God's grace and become His child and friend, He wants you to help others do the same. In fact, He plans to show the world who He is and what He's like through you.

> **The problem**—We rely too much on God working apart from us.
> **The reason**—Down deep, we don't want to take responsibility for our actions, or for the chaos around us.
> **The solution**—Submit to God, walk with Him, and see how He will use you to positively impact the world.

Even though God is more than capable of working on His own, a primary way He accomplishes His plans is actually through us. Never forcing us, He uses those who are submitted, acting in conjunction with their wills. As we give ourselves to Him, God fills us with His Holy Spirit, enabling us to live lives that represent Him. I referenced this before, but it bears repeating:

> *For those who are led by the Spirit of God are the children of God. The Spirit you received does not make you slaves, so that you live in fear again; rather, the Spirit you received brought about your adoption to sonship.*
>
> ROMANS 8:14-15 NIV

When I was angry at God, I didn't realize how He was

using all the people around me. My mother's prayers, the email from an old high-school friend saying God put me on his heart, and the acquaintance who invited me to church, were just a few of the means God used to redeem me. Once I became His child, even with all my old flaws, I saw Him now working through *me* for good in other's lives.

I stumbled into this at first, letting God bless people through me. But over time, I grew in recognizing if I allow God to use me, He will help people in ways which have everlasting effects. In the gospels, Jesus gave us a few "great" things to do. Christians refer to them as:

The great commandment,

"'You must love the Lord your God with all your heart, all your soul, and all your mind.' This is the first and greatest commandment. A second is equally important: 'Love your neighbor as yourself.' The entire law and all the demands of the prophets are based on these two commandments."

MATTHEW 22:37-40 NLT

And the great commission,

"Go and make disciples of all the nations, baptizing them in the name of the Father and

of the Son and of the Holy Spirit, teaching
them to observe all things that I have
commanded you; and lo, I am with you
always, even to the end of the age."

MATTHEW 28:19-20 NKJV

At the end of 2015, my wife and I started feeling nudges by God to take these "greats" of loving God, loving people, and making disciples seriously and practically. So we prayed and followed God's direction, which led to us moving our family about six short months later. You may assume it was to a foreign land, but it was just 9.8 miles down the road. We found ourselves in an apartment community with the purpose of blessing our neighbors and sharing the love of God.

We were aware of this goal each time we set foot outside our door, watching for opportunities God gave us, sometimes avoiding them out of fear, sometimes missing them and realizing too late, and sometimes getting to see God touch a life through us. We resolved to continue loving our neighbors whether we felt scared, tired, or incapable. After two years, we've gotten to plant seeds of faith with hundreds of people, and even seen tangible fruit from our labor.

We've been a part of eternal change—like the young girl recommitting her life to Christ, several families connecting with God and the church, and hearts we thought would never be open becoming softened towards our heavenly Father. While we may not know what other ways God has used us in this time, what's most important is that we've obediently walked with Him in love.

In early 2018, God called us to take another step towards fulfilling the great commission, and become involved with international missions. We stepped out of our comfort zone, packed up our bags and went to a missions training school run by former YWAMers in Montana with a focus on helping orphans and prostitutes be freed and protected from modern-day slavery. The school combined equipping and outreach in Montana, Germany, Latvia, and Amsterdam.

We believe God is calling us to help people see He loves them, chooses them, restores them, and has a purpose for their lives. At the time of writing this we've completed the training and are praying about which foreign land we're supposed to take the gospel to for a longer stay. It was a leap of faith to leave the comfort of our family, home, and local church (which we love and is where I have worked for almost three years). But we're excited to follow God's leading and are expecting Him to do great things! If you'd like to hear what we've been up to, and find out how to support us in prayer or financially check out the Additional Notes section following this chapter.

God desires to use you in powerful ways to help others as well. As the Holy Spirit leads you, you will fulfill the purposes of His heart. It may not be to work as a missionary, preach, or write a book about God, but He will show you how He desires to bless people through you. As you perceive Him and respond to Him with a submitted will, He will begin to change you and the world around you.

Reflect God

As you pursue God, He will change your perspective, thoughts, and feelings. He will continue to amaze you with how close He is and how loving He is. God is with you always, and He never stops loving you. He wants good things for you, but He won't force them on you. You will experience the blessings He has to offer you, as you walk in relationship with Jesus, and He changes you to be more like Him.

In Exodus 33, Moses asked God to show him His glory. Human eyes could not behold so much greatness, but God let the man see part of Him. As He passed by, God put His hand in front of Moses so he only saw His back. God's presence and goodness, in this brief moment, made Moses's face literally shine. In a similar way, if you spend time with God, a figurative light will radiate from you for the world to see.

> *"You are the light of the world—like a city on a hilltop that cannot be hidden. No one lights a lamp and then puts it under a basket. Instead, a lamp is placed on a stand, where it gives light to everyone in the house. In the same way, let your good deeds shine out for all to see, so that everyone will praise your heavenly Father."*
>
> MATTHEW 5:14-16 NLT

God accomplishes His will on Earth as His children read the Bible, pray, speak, and act in agreement with Him. In other words, God gets things done through born-again believers who listen to Him and obey Him. When we do this, we are changed into a reflection of God for the world to see.

Do Christians perfectly represent Him? No, but that doesn't stop Him from shining His light through us. Can God work apart from people? Yes, He can do whatever He wants. But we should not let that make us lazy, as if He is going to do everything without us. He tells us what to do through His Word and the Holy Spirit. We shouldn't excuse ourselves from living a life as His ambassador.

God provided the way for you to come to Him, through

Jesus. Using that freedom and the righteousness you've received in Christ, live your life according to His plans. Often I pray, "God, help me receive everything You have for me, and nothing the enemy has for me." What God makes available to us is free, but we must choose to take part in His gifts. I hope you will let God show the people around you, He's closer and more loving than they could ever imagine!

God Speaks

In our friendships, one person doesn't do all the talking. They listen and share thoughts. Yet many Christians do all the speaking in their relationship with God. He speaks to people today like He did in the Bible. He wants to talk with His people, but a lot of Christians don't believe or recognize He still speaks to us, so they never allow time to hear Him.

Ask God to speak to you, believe—and even expect—He will. In your devotional time, wait for Him to speak. Quiet your mind and listen. When He does, it will be in line with the truth of the Bible and His character of love, mercy, grace, and goodness. If He calls you to do something, it will lead to positive change. Trust and obey Him. As you step out in faith, your relationship with God will deepen and you'll see His generous blessings.

I'm currently writing a book on how to hear God communicate with us, a key element in living a life of adventure with God. It will cover different ways God speaks to us, what we can do to better hear Him, and what to do when He speaks. I've recorded a free teaching on this topic, which is available now. You can find the link to it and other free items in the Additional Notes section following this chapter.

In closing, despite the horrible things we see and experience in this life, God will always be with us. He's been by our sides, hoping we will lean on Him for comfort and peace. He loves each person immeasurably. Continue this journey of receiving His love and sharing it with others. God bless you richly!

Let's Pray...

God, I submit myself to You. Do whatever You want to do with me. I give up living my own way, and blaming You when things don't work out. Show me Your way. Show me how You've never left me, and You've always loved me. Show me Your glory. I will wait for You to reveal Yourself to me. I will seek You and give You room to speak into my life. I will talk to You and expect You to talk to me. Help me to follow You all the days of my life. I love You, God. I pray all this, in Jesus' name. Amen.

Next Steps:

1. When you give your life to God through Jesus's free gift of salvation, the Bible says you become a new creation (2 Corinthians 5:17). Living as a new creation should look differently than your previous life. As you continue to read the Bible and talk with God, believe the things He says about who you are and how you should live. We talked about this a bit in the Next Steps of Chapter 6, but it's worth mentioning again, because what He says seems impossible, we often gloss over it or dismiss it. But the life we are called to live is for today, not just for the future, so receive His Word and act on it now. This is how God changes everything.

2. God wants to speak into your life. You can learn to receive God's personal words for you and follow His guidance. Ask Him to speak to you, believe He will, start listening, and follow Him! Be sure to get my free audio teaching on hearing God (linked below) for more insights on this. Jesus said He did only what He saw His Father doing (John 5:19). He was in perfect communication with God always. We also need to learn how to see and hear what our heavenly Father is doing and saying.

3. No matter what the world, the enemy, or even your own mistakes bring you, never give up the belief that

God is with you and loves you deeply. Trust Him, walk with Him, and talk with Him. Let Him change you and change the world through you—for your good, the good of the world, and for His glory!

Additional Notes

I hope my words have blessed you. If they have, there are a few ways you can be even more blessed, forward the blessing to someone else, and help me at the same time. Check out all the free stuff I have for you below and find out how to partner with me and my family.

Who Needs to Hear this Message?

Take a moment and ask God to show you who else this book could help. He may bring someone to your mind that is going through a hard time, or struggling with questions about life and God. You have an opportunity to be a part of helping God use this book to draw them near to Him.

Be sure to let them know they can get this ebook, the accompanying workbook and journal, audiobook, and PDF on salvation and the gift of the Holy Spirit for free here:

GodAndYouAndMe.com/God-is-Here-Free-Stuff

Reviews are a Huge Help to Authors

Another way to help is with a few minutes of your time by leaving a quick review wherever you got this book. Reviews really help people to know if they should check out a book. You can review it on Amazon, Good Reads, Barnes & Noble, iBooks, Kobo, and/or Google Play Books. Please take a couple of minutes to review this book on one or more of these sites. I appreciate your feedback, so I can learn to communicate God's heart better, and hopefully reach more people. Thank you in advance!

More Free Books!

If you're interested in being an advance reader and have the opportunity to get future books for free, visit:

GodAndYouAndMe.com/Advance-Reader

Free MP3 Download on Hearing God

If you want my free audio teaching on hearing God, the common ways He speaks, and what to do when you've heard Him, go here:

GodAndYouAndMe.com/Hearing-God

Updates and Partnering with My Family

If you'd like an update on what God is doing with me and my family, and would like to support us in prayer or financially visit:

GodAndYouAndMe.com/Ministry-Partner

My Contact Information

Check out the About the Author chapter below for a bit more info about me and my family, as well as how you can contact me, connect on social media, and receive encouraging blog posts on my website.

References

1. Keller, Helen. *The Open Door.* New York: Doubleday, 1957. Print.

2. "Martin Luther King, Jr. Quotes." *Quotes.net.* STANDS4 LLC, 2018. Web. 14 Aug. 2018. https://www.quotes.net/quote/2537.

3. Alcott, Louisa May. "Through the Mist." *Work: A Story of Experience.* Boston: Roberts Brothers, 1873. Print.

4. "Three in Four Americans Believe in Paranormal" *Gallup.com.* Gallup Inc, 2018. Web. 14 Aug. 2018. https://news.gallup.com/poll/16915/three-four-americans-believe-paranormal.aspx.

5. Lewis, C.S. The Lion, the Witch, and the Wardrobe : A Story for Children. New York: Macmillan, 1950. Print.

6. "Plato Quotes." *Brainyquote.com.* BrainyQuote, 2018. Web. 14 Aug. 2018. https://www.brainyquote.com/quotes/

plato_121792.

7. Augustine. *Confessions,* translated by Rex Warner. New York: Mentor, 1963. Print.

8. "Saint Augustine Quotes." *Brainyquote.com.* BrainyQuote, 2018. Web. 14 Aug. 2018. https://www.brainyquote.com/quotes/saint_august ine_105351.

9. Eldredge, S. [StaciEldredge]. [Facebook Status Update]. Retrieved from https://www.facebook.com/StasiEldredge/posts/th ere-is-no-more-devastating-blow-against-evil- then-when-a-human-being-chooses- g/883243925155116/.

10. Scripture quotation taken from the *Amplified*® *Bible* (AMP), The Lockman Foundation, 2015. Used by permission. *Lockman.org.*

11. "30 Francis Frangipane Quotes." *ChristianQuotes.info.* Telling Ministries LLC, 2018. Web. 14 Aug. 2018. https://www.christianquotes.info/quotes-by- author/francis-frangipane- quotes/#axzz5OA5ycoKs.

A T THE MENTION OF books John W. Nichols ears perk up, he gets a spine-tingling sensation (no pun intended), and he can't help but find out what read is on discussion. With his first computer at twelve years of age, John began writing, and he is an avid reader, always with a stack of books by his bedside and listening to as many audiobooks as possible when working on mindless tasks. When Jesus saved him at the age of twenty, John started reading the best book you could ever read, over and over, recognizing the Holy Bible as a letter from the Creator of all things.

He thought one day (when he was old) he might write a book for God. But God thought he should write something sooner, and told John in a prayer session on January 1st, 2016 to write his book. Since then John has written several drafts of books and completed the one you are reading.

In other prayer sessions, God called John to preach His Word, seek His face, and go into the land He would show Him. He and his wife, Trinna, and three children, are following this call to show the love of Christ to the world. This was first exhibited teaching and leading worship in their local church, then by working with people with disabilities, then going to preach at the state prison, loving their neighborhood community, and now reaching out to women and children enslaved in human trafficking.

When John caught a glimpse of how God saw him, everything changed, and he has since sought to show others this good news. He's recognized most people, Christian or not, feel unfulfilled and don't know their life's purpose. This has led John to help people find their calling and have a life of adventure with God. To be encouraged in the way God sees you, and to keep up with what God is doing with John and his family, go to:

Godandyouandme.com

You can also connect with John in the following ways.
Email:
John@GodAndYouAndMe.com
Short words of encouragement:
GodAndYouAndMe.com/Blog

Social Media:

Facebook.com/GodAndYouAndMeBlog

YouTube.com/channel/UCqG-
TKZgn2PwwEQx9WlThoA

Istagram.com/Nichols_JohnW

Twitter.com/Nichols_JohnW

Linkedin.com/in/GodAndYouAndMe

GoodReads.com/author/show/18325435.John_W_Nichols

Amazon.com/author/Nichols_JohnW

Printed in Great Britain
by Amazon

51115269R00074